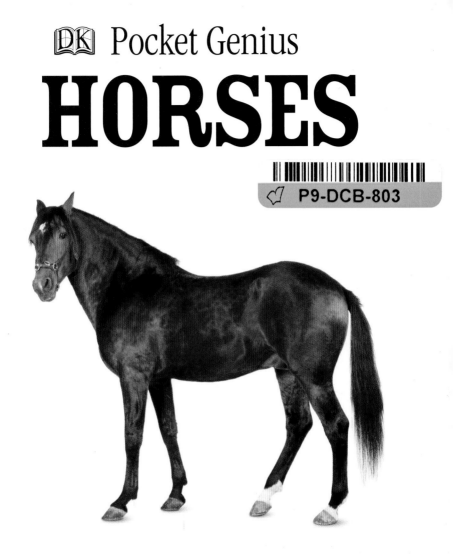

DK Pocket Genius

HORSES

P9-DCB-803

FACTS AT YOUR FINGERTIPS

LONDON, NEW YORK, MUNICH,
MELBOURNE, and DELHI

DK DELHI
Project editor Bharti Bedi
Project art editor Vikas Chauhan
Senior editor Samira Sood
Senior art editor Govind Mittal
Assistant editor Suneha Dutta
DTP designers Syed Mohammad Farhan, Jaypal Singh Chauhan
Picture researcher Sakshi Saluja
Managing editor Alka Thakur
Managing art editor Romi Chakraborty
CTS manager Balwant Singh
Production manager Pankaj Sharma

DK LONDON
Senior editor Fleur Star
Senior art editor Rachael Grady
US editor Margaret Parrish
US senior editor Rebecca Warren
Jacket editor Manisha Majithia
Jacket designer Laura Brim
Jacket manager Sophia M. Tampakopoulos Turner
Production editor Lucy Sims
Production controller Mary Slater

Publisher Andrew Macintyre
Associate publishing editor Liz Wheeler
Art director Phil Ormerod
Publishing director Jonathan Metcalf

Consultant Dr. Kim Dennis-Bryan

TALL TREE LTD.
Editor Jon Richards
Designer Ed Simkins

First American Edition, 2013

Published in the United States by
DK Publishing
375 Hudson Street
New York, New York 10014

13 14 15 16 17   10 9 8 7 6 5 4 3 2 1
001–187507–Jun/13

Published in Great Britain by Dorling Kindersley Limited.

A catalog record for this book
is available from the Library of Congress.

ISBN: 978-1-4654-0881-5

DK books are available at special discounts when purchased in bulk
for sales promotion, premiums, fund-raising, or educational use. For
details, contact: DK Publishing Special Markets, 375 Hudson Street,
New York, New York 10014 or SpecialSales@dk.com

Printed and bound in China by South China Printing Company

**Discover more at
www.dk.com**

CONTENTS

Scales and sizes

This book contains scale drawings
of horses to show how tall they are.
A horse's height is measured in hands.
One hand is equal to 4 in (10.16 cm).
The measurement is taken from a horse's
feet to the top of its shoulders (withers).

6 ft
(1.8 m)

The horse

Horses are grazing animals that are naturally adapted to run fast and have good endurance. These qualities led humans to domesticate horses thousands of years ago, breeding them to do specific jobs. Today, horses are also bred to produce animals with particular features, colors, and characteristics.

Long muzzle contains continually growing teeth

Withers (highest point of shoulders)

Vertebral column (spine)

Shoulder blade

Ribs protect heart and lungs

Belly

Hindquarters (area above hind legs)

Foreleg

Hind leg

Knee

Cannon (bone between knee and fetlock)

Hoof (foot of horse)

Fetlock

Anatomy

Although horses come in different sizes, shapes, and colors, they all have the same basic skeleton. A horse's back is straight, strong, and fairly rigid, making it suitable for riding and carrying heavy loads. A horse does not have any muscles below its knees and hocks. This saves energy, giving the animal better endurance. It has a single-toed hoof on each leg. A horse's height is measured in hands— one hand is 4 in (10.16 cm).

Girth (circumference measure behind withers around body's lowest part)

The Thoroughbred has the perfect conformation for speed

Thigh bone

Hock (joint on hind leg)

Conformation

The proportions and shape of a horse's skeleton, as well as its muscle development, are together known as its conformation. This varies with every breed and makes certain horses suitable for certain kinds of work. For example, the conformation of a horse that does heavy farmwork is usually different from that of a horse used for riding.

CONFORMATIONAL FAULTS

Some horses may have faults in their conformation, which may make them more likely to suffer from back injuries, lameness, or other problems.

A **sway back** is when there is a distinct dip in the spine behind the withers, giving the horse a U-shaped back.

Cow hocks occur when the lower hind legs slope outward due to closely set hocks.

When the forelegs are farther apart at the hooves than at the chest, it can cause the horse to throw one, or both, of its legs forward and to the side as it moves. This type of movement is known as **dishing**.

A horse with **pigeon toes** has inward-pointing hooves, which damage the joints in the legs.

In **splay feet**, the front hooves point outward. When the horse moves, its fetlocks strike each other.

Colors

Horses' coats come in a variety of colors. Some breeds have specific colors, while others have a range of colors. Most breeds retain the same coat color all their life, but a few develop new colors as they grow old. The Lipizzaner, for example, is born black but gradually turns gray as it ages.

Coat colors

Coat colors may be solid (of a single color), solid but with a different colored mane and tail, part-colored (any coat with white patches), or spotted.

A golden brown coat, mane, and tail is called **sorrel**.

Liver sorrel is the darkest shade of sorrel.

Gray is black skin with a mixture of white and black hair.

A black and white horse is **piebald**. A horse that is any other color, such as brown, and white is **skewbald**.

Flea-bitten is a gray coat with brown specks of hair.

APPALOOSA

Appaloosa coloring, also known as spotted coloring, has five main coat patterns: blanket (white coloring on the hips, with or without spots); leopard (a white coat with dark egg-shaped spots); snowflake (spots all over the body, concentrated on the hips); frost (white specks on a dark coat); and marble (a red or blue roan coat, with dark edges and a frost pattern in the middle). A number of other breeds also have spotted patterning.

Leopard coat pattern

Blue roan is a black or black-brown coat with white hair, which gives it a bluish tinge.

Red roan is a bay or bay-brown coat with white hair, which gives it a red tinge.

Black means the coat, mane, tail, and limbs are all black.

Brown is a mixed black and brown coat with a black mane, tail, and limbs.

Bay is a reddish brown to dark golden coat, with a black mane, tail, and lower limbs.

Dun is a brown-gray coat, ranging from yellow to blue-gray, all on black skin.

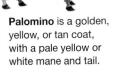

Palomino is a golden, yellow, or tan coat, with a pale yellow or white mane and tail.

Dapple gray is a gray coat with rings of dark hair, called dapples.

Markings

Most horses are not a single color, but have a variety of markings. These may be natural markings on the face, hooves, and legs, or acquired markings, such as brand and freeze marks, given to them by their owner.

Face markings

Horses often have white markings of various shapes on their face. Some common face markings are a star (a star-shaped marking between or just above the eyes); a blaze (a wide strip down the middle of the face); and a stripe (a narrow strip down the middle of the face). Some horses have a snip (a small strip on the muzzle, between the nostrils) or a white face (white hair covering almost the entire face).

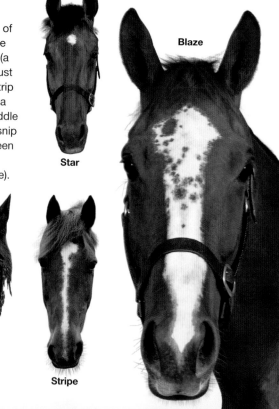

Star

Blaze

White face

Snip

Stripe

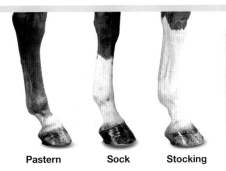

Pastern	Sock	Stocking

Leg markings

Many horses have markings on one or more of their legs. There are two main types: a sock, in which white hair covers the fetlock and part of the cannon bone; and a stocking, in which white hair covers the legs from the hoof to the knee or hock. A pastern is a white marking just above the hoof.

Primitive markings

Dun-colored horses often have a dark stripe stretching from their withers to their tails. They may have retained this feature from their early ancestors. Dun horses may also have horizontal striping on their lower legs, known as zebra bars.

Dorsal stripe

Zebra bars

Dark	Light

Hoof colors

Usually, a horse with white hair above the hoof has a light hoof, while one with dark hair has a dark hoof. Some hooves have vertical stripes.

ACQUIRED MARKINGS

A **freeze mark** is a unique identification mark made using an iron cooled in liquid nitrogen. This kills the pigment in the horse's hair, turning it white.

A **brand** can also be applied to indicate ownership or the breed of an animal. It is made by using a hot iron, which burns the mark on the skin of the horse.

Evolution

Modern horses have evolved over millions of years from animals that were very different. Their earliest known ancestor, *Hyracotherium*, was a browsing animal (one that eats leaves and fruits) that lived in forests 55 million years ago (mya). Modern horses are grazing (grass-eating) animals whose natural habitat is grasslands.

Evolution

This illustration shows some important stages in the evolution of the horse. As the horse evolved from being a browser to a grazer, its cheek teeth became broader and grew continually, since they were constantly being worn down. The muzzle became longer to hold the teeth.

Merychippus (25–20 mya) was a grass-eating horse. Although it had three toes, it ran only on its central toe. Aside from this, it looked like a modern horse.

Miohippus (32–25 mya) marked the point where horses started to diversify. It had a longer skull and limbs than previous horses.

Mesohippus (37–32 mya) had three-toed hooves, with the central toe bearing most of the weight.

Hyracotherium (55–45 mya) was a browsing woodland animal no bigger than a large dog. It had four toes on its front feet and three on the back.

Hyracotherium
16 in (40 cm)

Mesohippus
24 in (60 cm)

Miohippus
30 in (75 cm)

Merychippus
35 in (90 cm)

EVOLUTION OF THE HOOF

Hyracotherium had four toes on its front legs, although only three bore its weight. Over time, the number of toes reduced until, around 15 million years ago, the first single-toed horses evolved. Having just a single toe made the leg lighter as it requires fewer muscles, which improved the horse's endurance. Longer limbs increased the horse's stride length, making it faster.

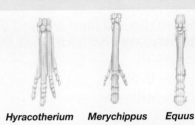

Hyracotherium   **Merychippus**   **Equus**

Pliohippus (12–6 mya) bore its weight on its central toe. Its other toes had almost disappeared.

Equus (5 mya–present) is the scientific name for all modern horses, including this domesticated horse. It has a single toe.

Pliohippus
4 ft (1.22 m)

Equus
4½–5 ft (1.4–1.5 m)

The horse family

Horses have several close relatives, including wild animals such as zebras, and domestic ones such as mules and donkeys. Together, they form the Equidae family and are known as equids.

Mountain zebra

Zebras

Zebras have a distinctive coat pattern of black and white stripes, which is unique to each zebra. There are three modern species of the zebra—the plains zebra, the mountain zebra, and the Grévy's zebra. Unlike horses, zebras have never been successfully domesticated.

Onagers

There are several other species of wild equid, including the onager. Native to the Middle East and central and south Asia, it is smaller than domesticated horses but has longer ears. It has a straight back, wispy tail, and thin legs.

Onager

Donkey

Descended from wild equids, the donkey has now been domesticated. It has great strength and stamina, and it is often used for herding and farmwork and to carry heavy loads over long distances.

Donkey

Mules and hinnies

Mules and hinnies are produced by crossing horses and donkeys. A mule is the product of a mare (female horse) and a male donkey, while a hinny is the product of a stallion (male horse) and a jenny (female donkey). These crossbreeds are mainly used for carrying goods.

Mule

Domestic horse

Domesticated horses

Wild horses were domesticated 6,000 years ago in Asia and eastern Europe. They were bred by humans for specific purposes, including heavy work such as plowing and sports such as racing. Horses used in farming and industrial work are generally called work horses. They are typically stronger and of a heavier build than sport horses, which are lighter, faster, and more athletic, making them more suitable for being ridden.

The domestic horse

The only surviving species of the wild horse is the Przewalski's horse, which lives in Mongolia. Most other horses are domesticated, which means they have been selectively bred by humans to perform certain tasks. Horses that have been bred to have the same set of characteristics are known as a "type," such as light horses and heavy horses. By breeding similar types of horse with one another, a consistent variety may be produced, known as a "breed."

Ponies

Typically, horses smaller than 14.2 hands are called ponies. Most ponies originated in harsh environments that provided little nutrition, which is why they are smaller than light and heavy horses. They are also tough, steady, and sure-footed and have coats that allow them to live outside all year round.

Light horses

Light horses are usually 14.2–16 hands tall. They are mainly used as riding horses, being faster and more athletic than most ponies and heavy horses. Their light bodies and long legs give them speed, so they are often used for racing and other sports.

HOTBLOODS, COLDBLOODS, AND WARMBLOODS

Horses are sometimes grouped by the region where they originated. Horses that came from desert areas are called **hotbloods**. They usually have a fiery nature. Most light horses are hotbloods.

Coldbloods came from the colder northern regions of the world. They are heavier, stronger, and slower than hotbloods and typically have a gentle nature. Most heavy horses are coldbloods.

Horses that are produced by crossbreeding hotbloods and coldbloods are known as **warmbloods**. They have the speed and agility of hotbloods but typically have a calmer nature.

Heavy horses

Breeds taller than 16.2 hands are known as heavy horses. Most are coldbloods and are generally larger and heavier than warmbloods and hotbloods. Being very muscular and strong, they are used for pulling heavy loads. Many have feathering—long hair growing on their lower legs.

Work horses

Ever since they were domesticated, horses have been used for pulling heavy loads, for transportation, and in battle. After the invention of machines and vehicles powered by steam and electricity in the 19th century, the demand for work horses decreased. However, they are still used in ceremonial parades, on some farms, and by police forces and armies.

Policing

Today, horses are used by several police forces, including those in the US, the UK, and Canada. Mounted police officers use specially trained horses to patrol busy streets. Horses are also used to control crowds because they are large and provide clear views to the riders.

Heavy work

Horses played an important role in the Industrial Revolution (1750–1850). They were used to provide power to machines, such as cotton-spinning frames, and to turn mill wheels to grind wheat or malt. They also hauled coal, a major source of energy for machines and vehicles, from mines.

Agricultural work

In some countries, horses are still used on farms for draft work—pulling vehicles or machines, such as those used for plowing or threshing. Many farmers still prefer horses to tractors, since they do not cause pollution, and their dung is a good fertilizer. They are also used for hauling heavy logs in forests.

Carriages

In past centuries, horse-drawn carriages were widely used for transporting goods and people and for postal services. Today, they are still used for certain activities, such as sightseeing tours and royal ceremonies. The activity of a horse pulling a vehicle to which it is harnessed (attached with straps and fittings) is called driving.

Sport horses

Horseback-riding, or equestrian, events have been popular since ancient times, and today are staged all over the world. In addition to the activities shown here, horses are used for show jumping, eventing, dressage, and polo.

Festivals

Several ancient equestrian sports are still performed at events and festivals around the world. For example, the Litang festival in China features tent pegging—in which competitors use lances to pick up targets from the ground—and reenactments of medieval-style jousts (horseback duels) are held in the US and the UK.

Gymkhanas

Gymkhanas are multigame horse-riding events that are usually organized for children. Events can include bending, in which a rider weaves through a row of poles. This is similar to barrel racing, in which a horse is maneuvered around a set of barrels.

Racing events

Horse races have been held for as long as people have been riding horses. Modern racing events usually involve galloping horses over a set distance, with or without obstacles for them to jump over. Other popular events include harness racing, in which a horse is harnessed to a small cart (called a sulky) in which a rider sits, and endurance races.

Performance

Some sports involve horses and riders being judged on their performance. In dressage, the suppleness, balance, and obedience of a horse are tested. In vaulting (below), gymnastics are performed on the back of a horse, which is judged on its movement.

Tent pegging

Gaits

Horses have four natural ways of moving, known as gaits. These are the walk, trot, canter, and gallop. Some breeds have specialized gaits, which include ambling or pacing. For example, the fox trot is the ambling gait of the Missouri Fox Trotter, and the running walk that of the Tennessee Walking Horse.

Natural gaits

One of the differences between the four natural gaits is the speed at which the horse travels. The walk has an average speed of 4 mph (6.4 kph); the trot, about 8 mph (13 kph); the canter, 10–17 mph (16–27 kph); and the gallop, 25–30 mph (40–48 kph). Gaits are also described by beats—the number of times each leg touches the ground in one cycle.

A **walk** is a four-beat gait in which the legs are placed on the ground one at a time. The hind leg is placed first, followed by the foreleg of the same side. The sequence is then repeated on the other side.

The **trot** is a two-beat gait in which the foreleg and hind leg diagonally opposite each other hit the ground at the same time. This step is then repeated by the other pair of diagonally opposite legs.

In the three-beat **canter**, one hind leg hits the ground first, followed by the other hind leg along with the foreleg diagonally opposite to it. The remaining foreleg hits the ground last.

The **gallop** is a four-beat gait in which one hind leg hits the ground first. This is followed by the other hind leg, the foreleg diagonally opposite to it, and finally, the remaining foreleg.

Behavior and communication

Horses are social animals. They live in groups called herds and communicate with each other mainly using body language and vocalization—making sounds with their vocal cords.

Play-fighting

Young horses often play-fight by rearing, biting, and kicking to establish dominance. These fights rarely result in any kind of injury.

Best range of vision

Blind spot

Best vision where ranges of left and right eye overlap

Range seen by left eye only

Range seen by right eye only

Blind spot

Eyes

Horses have large eyes set on the sides of their head. This gives them a wide range of vision, which helps them to look out for danger.

FLEHMEN

If a horse senses an unusual smell, it curls its top lip to draw more air into its mouth so it can analyze the smell with a special organ. This response is known as **flehmen**, and is also used by stallions to find out if a mare is ready for mating.

Ears

Horses have a highly developed sense of hearing. Each ear is controlled by 13 pairs of muscles and can be moved in different directions. The position of each ear is often a demonstration of a horse's mood.

One ear forward and one ear back means the horse is relaxed.

Both ears bent back may mean the horse is not happy.

Both ears forward means the horse is alert.

Mutual grooming

Horses that are well known to each other often bond through mutual grooming. This involves the animals standing head to tail and nibbling each other around the hindquarters and withers.

The Velká pardubická (Czech Republic) and the Grand Annual (Australia) each have

33 obstacles,

the highest number for any steeplechase

STEEPLECHASING
This event gets it name from horse races held in 18th-century Ireland. Riders rode through the countryside over uneven fields and other natural obstacles, using church steeples as course landmarks. Most races held today, such as the Velká pardubická shown here, are over artificial obstacles, such as brush fences.

Ponies

Usually, ponies are horses that measure less than 14.2 hands. Their small size is due to the fact that they evolved in harsh conditions where food was scarce. Ponies from cold climates developed thick coats, manes, and tails to adapt to their environments.

PONY TREKKING
Pony trekking is a popular sport all around the world. Riders follow trails and navigate their ponies around obstacles across rough and rocky terrains.

What is a pony?

A pony is a small horse, measuring less than 14.2 hands at the withers when fully grown. However, there are exceptions. In some cases, a horse more than 14.2 hands tall may be classified as a pony because of its proportions or local traditions.

Withers

Anatomy

Ponies usually have wider necks, shorter heads, and thicker manes than other horses. The body length of a pony is more than the height at its withers, and the depth of its girth equals the length of its leg. The length of a pony's head is equal to that of its shoulders.

Despite their small size, ponies are strong and can **pull heavy loads**. They are still used as pack animals (those that carry goods) in some places around the world.

Pony breeds

Mountain and moorland ponies, such as the Dartmoor Pony, are able to survive in harsh climates. Many European ponies, including Austria's Haflinger and the Norwegian Fjord, were once widely used for riding and driving. Some new breeds, such as the Ponies of the Americas, have been specifically developed for smaller riders.

GROOMING

Regular grooming keeps horses clean and healthy and helps riders bond with their horses.

▲ Brushing the coat removes dirt and dried mud. It also massages the body.

▲ It is important to pick out and shoe a horse's hooves regularly. Before a horse is shod, excess hoof growth is removed.

▲ The tail and mane are brushed to remove tangles and mud. A body brush is used to prevent hair breakage.

Ponies

Ponies are strong animals that were originally bred for driving and transporting goods and people. During the Industrial Revolution (1750–1850), they were used in coal mines as well. Today, they are mostly ridden for leisure, especially by children.

Icelandic Horse

This pony has one of the purest bloodlines because it has rarely been crossbred. There has been some selective breeding within the stock to enhance the five gaits it is noted for—walk, trot, canter, tolt, and pace.

SIZE   12.3–14.2 hands

ORIGIN   Iceland

COLORS   All colors

Deep girth

Gotland

Found on the Swedish island of Gotland since the Stone Age, this pony is believed to be the oldest Scandinavian breed. Its quick and active gait makes it suitable for jumping and trotting races.

SIZE	11.1–12.3 hands
ORIGIN	Gotland, Sweden
COLORS	Black, brown

Fjord

The Fjord has several primitive features, such as a dorsal stripe, zebra bars, and a mane that is traditionally cut so that the black hair at the center stands out. This sturdy pony is suitable for plowing and carrying heavy loads on remote mountain farms.

SIZE	13.2–14.2 hands
ORIGIN	Norway
COLORS	Dun, occasionally gray

Konik

The Konik has lived in Poland for centuries and has many primitive markings, including a dorsal stripe. This quiet breed is easily managed and useful for light agricultural work and haulage.

SIZE 12.3–13.3 hands

ORIGIN South and east Poland

COLOR Blue dun

Haflinger

A mountain pony, the Haflinger can move comfortably on steep slopes. It can be ridden and used in forestry work, or for drawing a sled or wheeled vehicle. In Austria, Haflingers, sometimes called Edelweiss ponies, have a brand mark featuring Austria's native flower, the edelweiss, with the letter "H" in the center.

SIZE 13.2–14.3 hands

ORIGIN Tyrol, Austria

COLORS Any shade of sorrel

Body is relatively long, but has a deep girth

Huçul

The Huçul, also called the Carpathian pony, came from the eastern Carpathian Mountains thousands of years ago. It is heavily built and has great endurance. For centuries, it was used for carrying heavy loads over difficult mountain paths. Now it is mainly used for light agricultural work and as a pack pony.

SIZE About 13.3 hands

ORIGIN Carpathian Mountains, Poland

COLORS All except white, dappled, and roan

Connemara

Ireland's only indigenous pony, the Connemara is now bred throughout Europe. Of all the mountain breeds, it is used the most in horse shows because it is an excellent jumper and performance pony. It can be ridden by adults as well as children.

SIZE 12.2–14.2 hands

ORIGIN Connemara, Ireland

COLORS All solid colors

Eriskay

Due to crossbreeding, the number of Eriskay ponies has reduced over time, and today only a few purebreds remain on the tiny island of Eriskay, in the United Kingdom. The breed is mainly used as a children's pony, for endurance riding, and for light draft work on the Scottish isles.

SIZE 12–13.2 hands

ORIGIN Outer Hebrides, Scotland

COLORS All colors

Highland

The tough Highland has lived for centuries in extremely harsh conditions. It is used for light agricultural and forestry work. A popular riding horse, it is also often used for trekking.

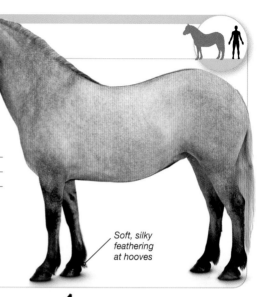

SIZE 13–14.2 hands

ORIGIN Highlands and islands, Scotland

COLORS All solid colors

Soft, silky feathering at hooves

Shetland

Despite its small size, the Shetland is one of the strongest of all horse and pony breeds. It can carry a rider over rough terrain and work under heavy loads. Shetlands are gentle and are often used for short rides in carnivals and fairs.

SIZE Up to 10.2 hands

ORIGIN Shetland Islands, Scotland

COLORS All colors, except spotted

Limbs are short and strong

Welsh Mountain Pony

This pony has the highest population of all the British mountain and moorland breeds. Because of its origins on wild uplands, it has evolved into an exceptionally powerful breed. It has a strong body, and, because it has been crossed with other breeds such as the Arab, it has a well-formed head.

SIZE	Up to 12 hands
ORIGIN	Wales
COLORS	All solid colors

Compact body with a deep girth

Welsh Pony

The Welsh Pony has the same small, pointed ears as the Welsh Mountain Pony and, like other Welsh breeds, it has a deep girth. However, its larger size makes it more versatile than the Welsh Mountain Pony. It also reflects features of other breeds, such as the Arab, with which it has been crossed in the past.

SIZE	Up to 13.2 hands
ORIGIN	Wales
COLORS	All solid colors

Dales

Initially developed as a pack pony, the sturdy Dales was used in mining and farmwork. The modern breed retains the strong bones and limbs of early Dales ponies, and its calm nature and sure-footedness make it popular for riding and trekking.

SIZE 14–14.2 hands

ORIGIN Eastern Pennines, England

COLORS Black, brown, gray, bay, roan

Short, powerful limbs with silky feathering

Fell

Like the Dales, the Fell was earlier used as a pack pony. Today, it is popular for riding and is commonly crossbred to produce competition horses.

SIZE Up to 14 hands

ORIGIN Western Pennines, England

COLORS Black, brown, bay, gray

Hackney Pony

First bred in the 1880s, the Hackney Pony is not to be confused with the Hackney Horse, since it displays genuine pony features. It has a light frame, a small head, and an arched, muscular neck. It is harnessed to pull light, two-wheeled vehicles.

SIZE 12.2–14 hands

ORIGIN Cumbria, England

COLORS Black, brown, bay, sorrel

New Forest Pony

The New Forest Pony is one of the larger native British breeds. This sure-footed animal is still used in the tough terrain of the New Forest. It is also used for dressage, gymkhanas, show jumping, and driving.

SIZE Up to 14.2 hands

ORIGIN New Forest, England

COLORS All colors except piebald, skewbald, and spotted

Long, sloping shoulders are well suited to riding

Lundy Pony

This is a fairly recent breed of pony, first developed in 1928 on the island of Lundy by the island's owner, Martin Coles Harman. It has a wide chest, strong legs, a muscular neck, and a compact back. Its gentle nature makes it popular among children.

SIZE Up to 13.2 hands

ORIGIN Lundy, England

COLORS Dun, gray, roan, bay, palomino, liver sorrel

Dartmoor

For centuries, the wild, hilly area where this pony is from has been easily accessible by land and sea. As a result, numerous breeds have been brought into the area and crossed with this pony. Today, few purebred Dartmoors remain on the moor (uncultivated hilly area).

SIZE Up to 12.2 hands
ORIGIN Dartmoor, Devon, England
COLORS Black, brown, bay, sorrel, gray, roan

Exmoor

The Exmoor is the oldest of the British mountain and moorland breeds. Because of the remoteness of its habitat, it was not crossbred often, so it has remained a relatively pure breed. It is a strong and powerful pony, suitable for long-distance riding and driving.

Deep girth

SIZE 11.2–12.3 hands
ORIGIN Exmoor, Somerset, England
COLORS Brown, bay, dun

Sorraia

A descendant of the
first primitive horses
to be domesticated in
Europe, the Sorraia still
has some features of its
wild ancestors. Its coat has
primitive markings, such as
the dorsal stripe and zebra bars. It also
has a large head and straight shoulders that
are typical of early horses, which were bred
specifically for these features.

SIZE	About 14.2 hands
ORIGIN	Plains of Sor and Raia, Portugal
COLORS	Light to dark dun

*Short legs
support compact,
robust body*

Landais

The Landais was originally a semi-wild pony. During World War II, it was crossed with heavier breeds to strengthen its build, so it is hard to find a purebred Landais today. After the formation of pony clubs in France in the 1970s, the Landais began to be bred selectively to meet the demand for children's ponies.

SIZE Up to 13.1 hands

ORIGIN Landes, France

COLORS Black, brown, bay, sorrel

Pottok

One of the few remaining native ponies of France, the Pottok is still semi-wild. Until World War II, it was used as a pack pony by smugglers in the Basque region. Today, it is in demand as a children's pony because of its obedient nature, although it has some conformational weaknesses, such as its short neck.

SIZE 11.1–14.2 hands

ORIGIN Basque region, France

COLORS Bay, brown, black, part-colored

Camargue

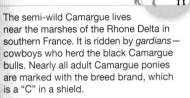

The semi-wild Camargue lives near the marshes of the Rhone Delta in southern France. It is ridden by *gardians*— cowboys who herd the black Camargue bulls. Nearly all adult Camargue ponies are marked with the breed brand, which is a "C" in a shield.

SIZE	Up to 14.2 hands
ORIGIN	Camargue, France
COLOR	Gray

Ariégeois

This tough breed can withstand even the harshest of cold weather. During Napoleon's French invasion of Russia in 1812, the Ariégeois coped with the difficult conditions much better than larger horses. Its feet are extremely hard, so it can work on steep, icy mountains, and travel long distances without horseshoes for protection.

SIZE	About 14.1–14.2 hands
ORIGIN	Eastern Pyrenees, France
COLOR	Black

PONY EXPRESS
In the mid-19th century, some areas in the US still used horse-drawn carriages to carry mail. The Pony Express, a relay horseback postal service started in 1860 between Missouri and California, cut down delivery time from weeks to days. It was stopped after the introduction of the telegraph in these areas.

The shortest time taken to cover the entire Pony Express trail of 2,000 miles (3,300 km) was

7 days and 17 hours

Bashkir

The Bashkir is able to survive even in subzero temperatures. It is bred as a pack and draft animal, as well as for its milk and meat. Its thick, curly winter coat can be cut and spun to make cloth.

SIZE About 14 hands

ORIGIN Russian Federation, northern Eurasia

COLORS Sorrel, bay, light brown

Skyrian Horse

Despite its small size, the Skyrian Horse, or Skyros, has proportions similar to a horse, and is an excellent jumper. Its coat is often marked with a dorsal stripe and zebra bars, and its feet are always black. Crossbreeding with feral donkeys from nearby areas has reduced the number of purebred Skyrians.

SIZE About 11.2 hands

ORIGIN Island of Skyros, Greece

COLORS Bay, dun, red-brown

Caspian

Despite its small size, the Caspian is an excellent jumper and runs as fast as much larger horses. Its narrow body makes it suitable for young riders.

SIZE Up to 12.2 hands

ORIGIN Arabian Peninsula, Middle East

COLORS All colors, except part-colored

Pindos Pony

A harsh climate has made the sure-footed Pindos Pony a tough breed that can live on very little food. It is used as a pack pony, for riding and driving, and for agricultural and forestry work. Known for its stamina, it is also very stubborn.

SIZE 13 hands

ORIGIN Thessalonika, Greece

COLORS Black, brown, bay

Batak

This pony is central to the life of the local Batak people from Indonesia. Aside from being bred for its meat, it is used for riding and racing. Its steady, calm nature and willingness to work make up for its weak bones and poor muscular development.

SIZE 12–13 hands

ORIGIN Central Sumatra, Indonesia

COLORS All colors

Tibetan Pony

Even though it has existed since ancient times, the Tibetan Pony was not officially recognized as a breed until 1980. In the past, these ponies were often sent as gifts to Chinese emperors. Today, they are mostly used as light draft animals, as well as for pack and riding work.

SIZE Up to 12 hands

ORIGIN Tibet

COLORS Mostly bay or gray

Sandalwood Pony

This pony is named after the sandalwood tree, which is Indonesia's main export. The biggest of the Indonesian ponies, it is used for riding, farm, and draft work, and for carrying loads. It is also used in harness racing and in Indonesia's famous bareback races, which can be up to 3 miles (5 km) long.

SIZE 12.2 hands

ORIGIN Sumba and Sumbawa Islands, Indonesia

COLORS All colors

Timor

The Timor is the smallest Indonesian pony breed. It is important for the island's economy, since it is used as a pack animal and for riding. It is also used by local herders to drive cattle.

SIZE 10–12 hands

ORIGIN Timor Island, Indonesia

COLORS All colors

Sumba Pony

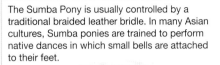

The Sumba Pony is usually controlled by a traditional braided leather bridle. In many Asian cultures, Sumba ponies are trained to perform native dances in which small bells are attached to their feet.

SIZE 12 hands

ORIGIN Sumba Island, Indonesia

COLORS All solid colors, dun

Java Pony

Because of its ability to withstand extreme heat, the Java Pony is especially useful in the tropical climate of the Indonesian island of Java. It is mainly used to pull *sados*—two-wheeled taxis that carry both goods and people. This breed is also ridden, and unlike other island ponies, its wooden saddle features toe stirrups—ropes with a knot at the ends for the rider's toes.

SIZE 11.2–12.2 hands

ORIGIN Java Island, Indonesia

COLORS All colors

Hokkaido Pony

One of Japan's few native breeds, the Hokkaido Pony is suitable for transportation and farmwork in the mountains, where other vehicles cannot pass. Some ranchers take their ponies to the mountains in the winter to maintain the breed's sturdiness. The ponies return to ranches in the spring by themselves.

SIZE 13–13.2 hands

ORIGIN Japan

COLORS Bay, black, sorrel, gray, roan

Tokara Pony

This breed was used for agricultural work, such as sugarcane processing. With the growing use of mechanical equipment, the demand for this pony dropped, and it stopped being bred. It is now an endangered breed, and despite efforts to increase its population, there are only about 100 Tokara ponies left in the world today.

SIZE 9.3–11.3 hands

ORIGIN Tokara Islands, Japan

COLOR Brown

Blue horn (blue or black) hooves

Australian Pony

Because Australia did not have any native horses, different breeds were imported for use by early settlers. The Australian Pony was developed from these breeds by 1920. With its smooth stride and well-angled shoulders, this pony is suitable for children and young riders.

SIZE Up to 14 hands

ORIGIN Australia

COLORS All colors

American Shetland

The American Shetland has no resemblance to its founding breed, the sturdy Shetland. It is longer and narrower and has more refined features. Well suited to being ridden by children, it is also used for show jumping, harness racing, and gymkhanas.

SIZE Up to 11.2 hands

ORIGIN US

COLORS All colors except spotted

Pony of the Americas

This pony was developed in 1954 by Leslie Boomhower of Mason City, Iowa, to provide a pony that was suitable for all children's activities. It has short, strong legs and hard feet that are not prone to diseases or damage from hard ground. These qualities make it ideal for ranch work, hunting, and endurance riding.

SIZE	11.2–14 hands
ORIGIN	Iowa
COLOR	Spotted

Galiceno

The Galiceno was popular for its smooth, steady running-walk, a gait that is still present in the modern Galiceno. Its comfortable gait and size make the Galiceno ideal for young riders moving from ponies to horses. Obedient and tough, it is used for ranch and farmwork, as well as for competition.

SIZE	Up to 14 hands
ORIGIN	Mexico
COLORS	All solid colors

Chincoteague Pony

There are only about 200 of these ponies left on the islands of Assateague (now a national park) and Chincoteague. These salty, sandy islands have little nutritious food. As a result, the breed suffered from several weaknesses, such as poor bone density and misshapen limbs. Crossbreeding has, however, improved the stock.

SIZE Up to 14.2 hands

ORIGIN Chincoteague and Assateague, Virginia

COLORS Most colors

Newfoundland Pony

In the past, this pony was used for plowing, hauling fish nets, gathering hay, and as transportation. Mechanization, however, reduced the demand for the Newfoundland Pony and it was not bred as often. There are fewer than 400 of these ponies today, and the breed is considered endangered.

SIZE 11–14.2 hands

ORIGIN Newfoundland, Canada

COLORS Black, brown, bay, sorrel, gray, roan, dun

PONY RACE
Shetlands are small, strong, and generally good-tempered, so they make great ponies for children. These Shetlands and their young riders are taking part in the Shetland Pony Grand National finals at the London International Horse Show. Riders must jump over fences up to 24 in (60 cm) high on horses that are just 3½ ft (1.03 m) tall.

Shetlands are the

strongest

of all horse breeds relative to their size and can pull loads twice their own weight

Light horses

Most horses that stand between 14.2 hands and 16 hands are categorized as light horses. Typically large and fast, they have a longer stride and a less rounded girth than ponies, which make them more comfortable for adults to ride. Some breeds are often crossbred to produce horses suitable for show and sports.

WESTERN RIDING
Cowboys in the Americas developed this riding style to suit their long working hours. The bridle and saddle are specially designed for cattle herding.

What is a light horse?

Light horses are fast and powerful with good stamina. In previous centuries, they were used in battle and to transport people rapidly from place to place, either by being ridden or pulling lightweight carriages. However, the introduction of new technologies, such as motor vehicles, reduced the demand for horses to perform these tasks.

Anatomy

A light horse has long legs, so the distance from its withers to the ground is more than the length of its body. Any horse with these proportions is classified as a light horse, even if it is less than 14.2 hands high.

SPORT HORSES

Light horses excel at sports. In **harness racing**, horses race against each other, pulling small, two-wheeled carts using either a trot or a pacing gait.

The withers are the highest point of the **shoulder** and should slope away gradually to the back.

Light horses

Bred for speed, light horses were mainly used to pull carts, for light draft work, and for riding. Today, these calm animals can be seen competing in a variety of sporting events and horse shows.

FOCUS ON...
LEGENDARY HORSES
Throughout history, horses have played an important part in war.

Swedish Warmblood

The Swedish Warmblood is larger than most light horses, and has strong shoulders, limbs, and joints. Bred originally for cavalry, it is now in demand as a competition horse for jumping, driving, and eventing. It is good-natured, which also makes it suitable for dressage.

SIZE 15.2–17 hands

ORIGIN Sweden

COLORS All solid colors

◀ Babieca was the war horse of Ruy Diaz, or El Cid—a Spanish hero who led the troops of Spain against the Moors.

◀ Bucephalus was the horse ridden by Alexander the Great in battle. After his horse died, Alexander founded the city of Bucephala, named after his beloved companion.

Døle Gudbrandsdal

The Døle Gudbrandsdal makes up almost half of Norway's horse population. It was originally used as a pack horse and in farming, but has since been crossbred with lighter breeds specifically to produce riding horses.

SIZE 14.2–15.2 hands

ORIGIN Gudbrandsdal valley, Norway

COLORS Black, brown, bay, sorrel

Finnish Horse

Originally, there were two breeds of Finnish Horse—the Finnish Draft and the Finnish Universal. The heavier Draft horse was a sturdy, powerful animal with quick, active paces. Since the 1970s, however, there has been a higher demand for the lighter Universal horse, which is used for riding, transportation, and harness racing. This breed is easy-going and has great stamina.

SIZE	15.2 hands
ORIGIN	Finland
COLORS	Mostly black, bay, sorrel

Knabstrup

The Knabstrup is known for its unusual leopard-spotted coat. Once popular as a circus horse, it was also used by Denmark during the Schleswig War (1848–50), fought against Germany.

SIZE	More than 14.2 hands
ORIGIN	Denmark
COLORS	Mostly spotted, but some solid colors

Danish Warmblood

A relatively new breed, the Danish Warmblood is a handsome horse with strong limbs. Its free action and excellent nature make it suitable for dressage and show jumping competitions.

SIZE About 16.2 hands

ORIGIN Denmark

COLORS All solid colors

Frederiksborg

Denmark's oldest breed, the Frederiksborg was developed at the Royal Frederiksborg Stud, founded in 1562 by King Frederik II. He wanted a breed that could be used in the army as well as in parade and court ceremonies. This lively horse, with an energetic action, was considered a mark of luxury and many Frederiksborgs were sold abroad, leading to the closing of the stud farm in 1839.

SIZE 15.3–16 hands

ORIGIN Denmark

COLORS Bay, sorrel, gray, dun, palomino

Wielkopolski

The Wielkopolski was bred by crossing two Polish breeds—the Poznan and the Masuren—that are now extinct. The horse is known for its different paces—long, easy walk; low, level trot; and fast canter and gallop.

SIZE	16–16.2 hands
ORIGIN	Central and western Poland
COLORS	All solid colors

Trakehner

Widely considered as Europe's finest warmblood, this competition horse is very good at dressage and show jumping. It was also a popular military horse. During World War II, 1,200 Trakehners were trekked 900 miles (1,450 km) across Europe to prevent them from falling into Soviet hands.

Strong, sloping shoulders

SIZE	15.2–16.2 hands
ORIGIN	Lithuania
COLORS	All solid colors

Irish Draft

This breed is often crossbred to produce sport horses. When crossed with the Thoroughbred, it produces the world's best cross-country horse—the Irish hunter.

SIZE	15.1–16.3 hands
ORIGIN	Ireland, UK
COLORS	All solid colors

Hind legs are powerful with strong thighs

Welsh Cob

The Welsh Cob is a larger version of the Welsh Mountain Pony. It was formerly used by the military and is still used for riding and driving. It is often crossed with the Thoroughbred to produce competition horses.

SIZE   More than 13.2 hands

ORIGIN   Wales

COLORS   All colors except piebald and skewbald

Hackney Horse

The modern Hackney has great stamina and can trot at high speeds for long periods. It is known for its high action, which makes it seem like the horse is floating. For these reasons, this breed is the most spectacular show-ring harness horse.

SIZE   More than 14.2 hands

ORIGIN   Norfolk, England

COLORS   Bay, dark brown, sorrel, black

Forelegs have an elevated action

Cleveland Bay

The Cleveland Bay is one of Britain's oldest and purest indigenous breeds. After World War II, their numbers declined and by 1962, there were only four stallions left in Britain. With only 500 purebreds left in the world, this breed remains on the Rare Breeds Survival Trust's critical list.

SIZE 16–16.2 hands

ORIGIN Cleveland, England

COLOR Bay

Powerful quarters help in jumping

Anglo-Arab

The Anglo-Arab was developed with the goal of combining the stamina of the Arab and the speed of the Thoroughbred. Although not as fast as the Thoroughbred, it has similar proportions that allow a strong gallop.

SIZE 15.2–16.3 hands

ORIGIN UK and France

COLORS All solid colors

Thoroughbred

One of the fastest and most valuable breeds in the world, the Thoroughbred forms the base of a huge racing industry. It is also the main horse used in crossbreeding to improve other breeds and produce competition horses.

SIZE 15–17 hands

ORIGIN England

COLORS All solid colors

Dutch Warmblood

This is one of the most successful competition breeds. It is athletic, with strong limbs and feet, and good at show jumping and dressage. Breeders of Dutch Warmbloods ensure that only horses of good conformation and action and calm nature are selected to be crossbred.

SIZE 16–17 hands

ORIGIN Netherlands

COLORS Black, brown, bay, gray

Gelderlander

The Gelderlander was bred with the goal of producing a horse suited for drawing carriages and capable of doing some light draft work. Its legs are short and strong, and it performs well in driving competitions.

SIZE 15.2–16.2 hands

ORIGIN Gelder province, Netherlands

COLORS Sorrel, bay, gray

Friesian

This breed performs best when in harness because it is energetic and has a well-balanced gait. Its black coat made it a popular carriage horse because it could easily be matched to other breeds.

SIZE 15–16 hands

ORIGIN Friesland, Netherlands

COLOR Black

Groningen

The Groningen has limited knee movement, so until 1945 it was used only for heavy farmwork. Due to an increased demand for active and versatile horses, however, it has been bred to be lighter and more compact. As a result, it hardly exists in its original form now.

SIZE 15.3–16.1 hands

ORIGIN Groningen region, Netherlands

COLORS Black, bay, sorrel, gray

Belgian Warmblood

Historically, Belgium has been known for breeding heavy horses for farmwork, and the Belgian Warmblood is a recent development aimed to produce competition horses. This agile breed is well suited to dressage and jumping.

SIZE 15.1–17 hands
ORIGIN Belgium
COLORS All colors

Bavarian Warmblood

This is one of the oldest known German warmbloods, with its origins dating back to the Crusades (1095–1291). The modern Bavarian Warmblood has strong, short legs. It is calm and easily manageable, so it is well suited to jumping and dressage competitions.

SIZE 15.2–16.2 hands
ORIGIN Rott Valley, Bavaria, Germany
COLORS All colors

Hanoverian

One of the most successful European warmbloods, the Hanoverian has a good reputation as a show jumper and dressage horse. A strict process of selection ensures that the breed has strength, correct movement, and an easy-going nature.

SIZE About 16.1 hands
ORIGIN Hanover, Germany
COLORS All solid colors

Westphalian

After the
Hanoverian,
the Westphalian
makes up the largest
population of warmbloods
in Germany. Its Hanoverian influences
make it ideal for sporting events,
including show jumping and dressage.

SIZE 15.2–17.2 hands

ORIGIN Germany

COLORS All solid colors

White horses were considered

sacred

by the Celtic tribes of

ancient Britain

UFFINGTON WHITE HORSE
Cut into the chalk hills of southern England, the 360-ft- (110-m-) long Uffington White Horse is at least 3,000 years old. This figure is believed to represent Epona, the Celtic horse-goddess of health, fertility, and death.

Mecklenburger

Until World War II, Mecklenburgers were bred as all-purpose utility horses. They worked as cavalry, transportation, and farm horses. The increase in the use of machinery after the war reduced the work of these horses, and they are now mainly bred for riding and sports.

SIZE 15.3 hands and above
ORIGIN Germany
COLORS Black, bay, sorrel, gray

Holstein

Originally a heavier breed, the Holstein worked as a coach horse. As the demand for riding horses increased, it was crossbred with the Thoroughbred. The modern Holstein has correct, straight, and rhythmic paces and is now used for dressage and show jumping.

Muscular thighs

SIZE 15.2–17 hands
ORIGIN Holstein, Germany
COLORS All solid colors

Oldenburg

The heaviest
of the German
warmbloods, the
Oldenburg was first developed
as a coach horse for journeys over
rough roads. Since then, it has been
selectively bred to suit changing
requirements and is now most often
a riding horse.

SIZE 16.1–17.2 hands
ORIGIN Oldenburg, Germany
COLORS All solid colors

*Thick legs with
short cannons*

Rhinelander

This heavy horse was once used in agriculture, but has since been crossbred to produce a lighter Rhinelander. This variety has an easy, steady nature and is well suited for leisure riding.

SIZE About 16.2 hands

ORIGIN Rhineland and Westphalia, Germany

COLORS All solid colors

Wurttemburg

The ancestors of the Wurttemburg were bred in the 17th century as utility horses that could be used for riding and light harness work. The modern Wurttemburg is athletic, with a conformation that makes it a successful show jumper in competitions.

SIZE About 16.1 hands

ORIGIN Marbach, Wurttemburg, Germany

COLORS Black, brown, bay, sorrel

Lusitano

The Lusitano has quick movements and great balance. It has a naturally high action and the demand for this cooperative and responsive breed has grown because it performs well in dressage and classical riding. Its agility and balance also made it popular with mounted bullfighters.

SIZE About 15.1–15.3 hands

ORIGIN Portugal

COLORS Mostly gray; also bay, black, dun, palomino, sorrel

Alter-Real

The Alter-Real gets its name from the town Alter de Chão, where it was first bred. *Real* means "royal" in Portuguese, and as the name suggests, this horse was bred for the royal stables, for classical riding, as well as for drawing carriages.

SIZE 15–16 hands

ORIGIN Alter, Portugal

COLORS Brown, bay, gray

Andalucian

The modern Andalucian is agile and athletic, with strong limbs and shoulders. Its mane and tail are often wavy.

SIZE 15.2–16.2 hands
ORIGIN Jerez, Spain
COLORS All except part-colored

Shoulders are strong and wide

French Trotter

This breed was developed for the sport of trotting, which was established in France in the early 19th century. It has powerful limbs and well-balanced gaits.

SIZE About 16.2 hands
ORIGIN Normandy, France
COLORS Mostly brown, bay, sorrel

Selle Français

The Selle Français was developed as a show jumper. This strong horse has an energetic movement and long stride and performs well in cross-country racing and eventing.

SIZE 15.2–17 hands

ORIGIN Normandy, France

COLORS All colors

Freiberger

This mountain-bred draft horse is active and sure-footed. For many years it was used as a pack animal and for agricultural work on small mountain farms. Today, this horse can also be used for driving, riding, eventing, and transportation.

SIZE 14.3–15.2 hands

ORIGIN Switzerland

COLORS Bay, sorrel

Quarters have powerful muscles

Shagya Arab

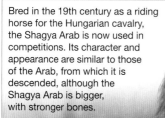

Bred in the 19th century as a riding horse for the Hungarian cavalry, the Shagya Arab is now used in competitions. Its character and appearance are similar to those of the Arab, from which it is descended, although the Shagya Arab is bigger, with stronger bones.

SIZE 15–16 hands

ORIGIN Babolna, Hungary

COLORS Gray, bay, sorrel, black

Nonius

When it was first bred in the 19th century, the Nonius had a weak conformation, including a heavy head, a short neck, and a low-set tail. Extensive crossing with Thoroughbreds has improved the Nonius, and it is now a good jumper and competition horse.

SIZE 15.1–16.1 hands

ORIGIN Hortobagy, Hungary

COLORS Black, brown, bay

Furioso

Also called the Furioso-North Star, this horse is named for the two horses used to produce it—Furioso, an English Thoroughbred, and North Star, descended from the Norfolk Roadster. Both stallions were bred with Nonius mares, and the two crossbred versions were intercrossed in 1885 to produce this breed.

SIZE 15.2–16.3 hands

ORIGIN Apajpuszta, Hungary

COLORS Bay, black, brown

Strong, compact body

Salerno

Once a popular cavalry breed, the Salerno is an expert riding horse and has a talent for jumping. Its Thoroughbred influence has given it a strong, elegant conformation, with excellent bones and feet.

SIZE	16–17 hands
ORIGIN	Campania, Italy
COLORS	Mostly black, bay, sorrel

Murgese

The Murgese is useful for light draft work and on farms. Despite some conformational weaknesses, such as a short stride and poorly developed quarters, it is a useful cross to produce good riding horses, because of its energetic movement and calm nature.

SIZE	14.3–16.2 hands
ORIGIN	Murge, Italy
COLORS	All solid colors

Sanfratellano

This semi-wild breed lives in the Nebrodi Mountain Park, Sicily. It is strong and muscular and is mainly used for riding and light draft work.

SIZE 14.3–15.3 hands
ORIGIN Sicily, Italy
COLORS Bay, black

Maremmana

Once bred for use by troops and the police, this versatile horse can also be used for agricultural and draft work. Italian herders use this breed to herd cattle.

SIZE 15.3–17 hands
ORIGIN Tuscany, Italy
COLORS All solid colors

Lipizzaner

Originally bred as a show horse for the nobility, the Lipizzaner is now used for riding, driving, and draft work, and the breed excels at classical dressage. While most horses have an average life span of 28 years, Lipizzaners are known to live well into their thirties.

SIZE 15.1–15.2 hands

ORIGIN Lipica, Slovenia

COLORS Mostly gray; also black, bay

Barb

Because of its historical and continued use in the production of most of the world's horses, the Barb is one of the founding breeds of the world's horse population. Originally used in the military, it is now often used in races and to produce other racing breeds.

SIZE	13.2–15 hands
ORIGIN	Morocco
COLORS	All colors

ROYAL HORSES

Elegant Lipizzaners are famous for their classic dressage skills. They perform haute école (high school) acrobatic movements, which require strength, control, and balance. The best place to see Lipizzaners perform is at the Spanish Riding School in Vienna, Austria. At more than 400 years old, it is the oldest riding academy in the world.

It can take

10 years

of training for a Lipizzaner stallion to be able to perform "airs above the ground" dressage

Kladruber

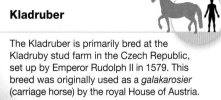

The Kladruber is primarily bred at the Kladruby stud farm in the Czech Republic, set up by Emperor Rudolph II in 1579. This breed was originally used as a *galakarosier* (carriage horse) by the royal House of Austria.

SIZE	15.2–16.3 hands
ORIGIN	Czech Republic
COLORS	Black, gray

The Czech Republic gave the UK's Prince William and Kate Middleton a Kladruber as a wedding present in 2011.

Karabakh

Originally from the steppe-mountains of Azerbaijan, this horse is used in mounted games, such as *chavgan*, a type of polo. It is the national animal of Azerbaijan, and is even featured on the country's postage stamps.

Long, slender limbs make the Karabakh suitable for racing

SIZE 14.2–14.3 hands

ORIGIN Azerbaijan, northern Eurasia

COLORS Bay or sorrel with metallic golden tint, gray

Czechoslovakian Warmblood

First used as a cavalry horse, this breed is today used in various sports competitions and for light agricultural work. Its calm nature makes it suitable for novice riders (those who are learning to ride).

SIZE 15.3–16.3 hands

ORIGIN Czech Republic

COLORS Mostly black, bay, sorrel

Akhal-Teke

A historically significant breed in Turkmenistan, where it is a national emblem, the Akhal-Teke was used in the military. These horses were often presented as gifts to the rulers of Russia in the 19th century. Bred in a harsh desert climate, the breed is noted for its stamina. Originally used by local desert tribesmen, it is now a sport horse.

SIZE 14.1–17 hands

ORIGIN Turkmenistan, northern Eurasia

COLORS Mostly bay and dun; black, sorrel, palomino, all with metallic sheen; also gray

In 1935, an Akhal-Teke herd completed a desert trail of 2,565 miles (4,128 km) in 84 days with little food and water.

Budenny

The Budenny is named after Semyon Budenny, a cavalry commander who set up the stud farms that led to the development of this breed in the 1920s. Originally intended as a Russian cavalry horse, today it is used in steeplechasing, endurance riding, and dressage.

SIZE	16–16.3 hands
ORIGIN	Russian Federation, northern Eurasia
COLORS	Mostly sorrel, bay

Tersk

This fast horse is excellent at endurance riding and flat racing. It is noted for its ability to survive in a harsh, cold climate despite its fine coat.

SIZE 14.3–15.1 hands

ORIGIN Northern Caucasus, northern Eurasia

COLORS Gray, bay, sorrel

Kabardin

This sure-footed mountain breed can easily cross steep passes and rivers, and travel in deep snow. Known for its good sense of direction, it can even find its way through thick mountain mist. It is used as a pack and riding horse.

SIZE 15–15.2 hands

ORIGIN Northern Caucasus, northern Eurasia

COLORS Black, bay

Don

Valued for its strength and ability to work in extremely cold climates, the Don was traditionally used by the cavalry, most famously by the Cossacks during the French invasion of Russia in 1812. It is strong and calm-natured but has some conformational weaknesses, including short shoulders that limit the length of the stride.

SIZE 16.1 hands

ORIGIN Russian Federation, northern Eurasia

COLORS Sorrel with metallic sheen, brown, bay

During battles, the Don was used to pull a *tachanka*, a cart with a machine-gun installed at the back.

Orlov Trotter

The Orlov Trotter was developed in the late 18th century by Alexei Orlov, a Russian aristocrat, who wanted a suitable horse for harness racing. This fast trotter is often used to pull a *troika*, a Russian horse-drawn vehicle. It is also increasingly being used to improve other breeds because of its height and strength.

SIZE 15.3–16 hands

ORIGIN Moscow, Russian Federation, northern Eurasia

COLORS Black, bay, sorrel, gray

Russian Trotter

The Russian Trotter has a muscular build and is easy to train, making it suitable for racing. Although its legs are powerful, its conformation is not as strong as that of the Orlov Trotter.

SIZE 15.2–15.3 hands

ORIGIN Russia

COLORS Mostly black, bay, sorrel; also gray

Arab

The Arab is one of the oldest breeds in the world, and its ancestors can be traced back to 2500 BCE. It has been used to improve many modern horse breeds. The most notable feature of the Arab is its slightly inward-curving face, called a dish face.

SIZE	14.1–15.1 hands
ORIGIN	Arabian Peninsula, Middle East
COLORS	Mostly bay, sorrel, gray; also black, roan

Marwari

The Marwari is a rare breed native to Jodhpur, India. Traditionally, the locals decorated it with jewels and bells, and trained it to dance at ceremonies, such as weddings—a practice that is still popular in rural areas. The breed's ability to perform also makes it suitable for dressage.

SIZE	14.2–15.2 hands
ORIGIN	Jodhpur, India
COLORS	All colors

Kathiawari

Used by several Indian state police forces, the Kathiawari is a strong horse that can survive on little food and water. It has highly flexible ears that, when pricked, curve inward to touch each other at the tips.

SIZE	About 15 hands
ORIGIN	Kathiawar province, India
COLORS	Gray, sorrel, all shades of dun

Australian Stock Horse

With immense stamina and strength, this breed is capable of carrying heavy weight and herding cattle and sheep all day. It was once used as a cavalry horse and exported to many countries for use in their armies. It is now used primarily as a riding horse.

SIZE	14–16 hands
ORIGIN	New South Wales, Australia
COLORS	Mostly bay

Lokai

This small but strong horse is used as a pack animal in the tough terrain of the Caucasus Mountains. It is also used for riding and in the local sport of *kokpar*, a game in which riders try and gain possession of a goat carcass.

SIZE	13–14.3 hands
ORIGIN	Tajikistan
COLORS	Mostly black, bay, sorrel, gray

Missouri Fox Trotter

This breed is known for its peculiar "fox trot" gait, in which it walks with an energetic action with the front legs while trotting with the hind legs. Its back remains stable while performing this gait, which makes this a comfortable riding horse.

SIZE 14–16 hands

ORIGIN Arkansas and Missouri

COLORS Black, brown, bay, sorrel, dun

Appaloosa

The Appaloosa is a spotted breed that has five coat patterns—leopard, snowflake, blanket, marble, and frost. Aside from its varied coloring, it is unique for being the only breed whose sclera—the white of the eyes around the iris—is visible.

SIZE More than 14.2 hands

ORIGIN US (established)

COLOR Spotted

Leopard coat

The official horse of the state of Idaho, the Appaloosa is featured on the license plate of its cars.

Palomino

This horse is technically a color-type and not a breed, since any horse with a golden coat and a white mane and tail is called a Palomino. When two Palomino horses are bred with each other, there is only a 50 percent chance that the foal will be of the same color.

SIZE	More than 14.2 hands
ORIGIN	US (established)
COLOR	Palomino

Quarter Horse

Famous for its short-distance sprinting, this breed is actually named for its excellence in quarter-mile races. It is also used for herding cattle and in rodeo competitions.

SIZE 14.3–16 hands

ORIGIN US

COLORS Most colors

Pinto

Like the Palomino, the Pinto is a color-type and not a breed. It gets its name from the Spanish word *pintado*, which means "painted." This breed has many coat patterns, of which the most common are the overo, a solid-color coat with white patches on it; and the tobiano, a white coat with patches of solid color.

White patches on overo coat are shaped like jigsaw puzzle pieces

SIZE	Variable
ORIGIN	US
COLOR	Part-colored

Araappaloosa

A cross between the Arab and the Appaloosa, this breed is noted for its stamina, sure-footedness, and color. It is suitable for endurance riding, shows, and ranch work.

SIZE	14–15 hands
ORIGIN	US
COLOR	Spotted

Bronc riding is a main rodeo event in which a rider tries to stay on a

bucking horse

for at least eight seconds

Morgan

The Morgan is a tough breed with strong quarters and feet. Because of its strength and stamina, it was used extensively by the US Army in the Civil War (1861–65), and today, it is used for hunting, jumping, dressage, and driving.

SIZE 14.1–15.2 hands

ORIGIN Massachusetts and Vermont

COLORS All colors, but mostly bay, sorrel

Colorado Ranger

The Colorado Ranger, or Rangerbred, was developed in 1878 by breeding an Arab and a Barb. The resulting horse was bred with trotting mares and later, the spotted color was introduced. This breed's strong limbs, compact body, and hard feet make it an excellent working horse.

SIZE 14.2–15.2 hands

ORIGIN Colorado

COLORS Black, bay, sorrel, gray, roan, spotted

Morab

The Morab gets its name from its two parent breeds, the Morgan and the Arab. It was developed in the 1880s as a carriage horse that could also do farmwork. Today, it is also used as a riding horse.

SIZE 14.1–15.2 hands

ORIGIN US

COLORS All colors except spotted

Tennessee Walking Horse

The Tennessee Walking Horse is known for its comfortable paces. Its three distinct gaits are: the flat walk in which it makes long, brisk strides, traveling at 4–8 mph (6–13 kph); the faster running walk, in which it increases its speed to 10–20 mph (16–32 kph); and the canter, in which riders are said to feel as though they are sitting in a rocking chair.

SIZE 14.3–17 hands

ORIGIN Tennessee

COLORS All colors

Standardbred

Standardbreds have powerful quarters, legs, and feet. They are used for harness racing, in which they either trot or pace, and can cover 1 mile (1.6 km) in under 2 minutes.

SIZE More than 14.2 hands

ORIGIN East Coast, US

COLORS Most colors

Rocky Mountain Horse

The Rocky Mountain Horse is noted for its smooth ambling gait, which is comfortable for riders across rough terrain. This sure-footed breed is often used for riding and carrying loads through the wild countryside of states such as Wyoming and Montana.

SIZE	14.2–16 hands
ORIGIN	Rocky Mountains
COLOR	Chocolate

The Peruvian Paso is considered part of the *patrimonio cultural* (cultural heritage) of Peru.

Campolina

The Campolina is named after its Brazil-based breeder, Cassiano Campolina. Its steady ambling gait makes it suitable for leisure riding, driving, and dressage.

SIZE	About 16 hands
ORIGIN	Brazil
COLORS	Most colors

Peruvian Paso

The Peruvian Paso has been specifically bred to develop its unique natural pace called the *paso llano*. This is a comfortable, smooth gait in which the forelegs swing outward from the knee. The Peruvian Paso can maintain this gait over long distances.

SIZE	14.1–15.3 hands
ORIGIN	Peru
COLORS	All solid colors, roan, palomino

Outward movement of forelegs

Criollo

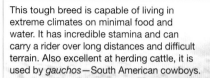

This tough breed is capable of living in extreme climates on minimal food and water. It has incredible stamina and can carry a rider over long distances and difficult terrain. Also excellent at herding cattle, it is used by *gauchos*—South American cowboys.

SIZE 13.3–15.1 hands

ORIGIN Argentina

COLORS All colors

Falabella

The smallest known Falabella in history was Sugar Dumpling, a mare that weighed 30 lb (13.6 kg) and stood 5 hands high.

The Falabella is the smallest of any domestic horse and pony breed. It was produced by crossing local Criollo horses with Shetlands and Thoroughbreds. Producing small horses consistently, however, led to inbreeding, which caused weaknesses in the Falabella's conformation. These horses are too small to be ridden and are mostly kept as pets.

SIZE	6.1–8.2 hands
ORIGIN	Buenos Aires, Argentina
COLORS	Most colors

The largest stadium for chariot racing in ancient Rome, the Circus Maximus could seat

250,000 people

CHARIOT RACING
Chariot racing was very popular in ancient Rome, where races were held between teams (or *factiones*). The four Roman racing teams were known by their colors—red, white, blue, and green. Red and blue teams can be seen in this 19th-century illustration of a race at the Circus Maximus.

Heavy horses

Before the invention of steam engines, heavy horses were the main source of power and were used for transportation, plowing, harvesting, and threshing. These coldbloods usually measure 16.2 hands or above and are bred for heavy draft and farmwork.

HAULING
Because of their size and strength, heavy horses are still used to pull loads in some areas, especially those where the terrain is unsuitable for machines.

What is a heavy horse?

Heavy horses are large draft breeds, suitable for farmwork and for hauling heavy loads, such as logs. They are often crossbred with light breeds to develop strong riding horses.

Anatomy

The typical heavy horse has a wide body with a broad back. Its quarters are wide and muscular, making it very strong. Most heavy horses also have feathering (long hair at the hooves). This helps to protect their legs and keeps them warm in the cold environments where they usually work.

The power of a heavy horse comes from the large muscles in its quarters that allow it to pull very heavy loads.

BREWER'S HORSE

Heavy horses played an important role in the **brewing industry** in the 1800s, particularly in the UK. They were used for driving water pumps, turning millstones, and pulling wagons loaded with beer barrels.

Heavy horses

The typical heavy horse has strong muscles, heavy bones, and a short, broad back. This conformation makes it suitable for haulage and draft work, although heavy horses are sometimes ridden as well.

North Swedish Horse

Compact and active, the North Swedish Horse is Sweden's only heavy horse breed. It is a powerful, tough horse and can pull heavy loads. It is used for farm and forestry work as well as for riding and driving.

Large head with long ears

SIZE 15–15.2 hands

ORIGIN North Sweden

COLORS Black, brown, sorrel, gray, dun, palomino

Jutland

Native to Denmark, this horse and its ancestors have been bred on the Jutland Peninsula for centuries. It is used in some areas for farmwork and for hauling heavy loads.

SIZE	15–16 hands
ORIGIN	Jutland Peninsula, Denmark
COLORS	Mostly sorrel; also black, brown, roan

Thick, coarse feathering

Noriker

The strong, sure-footed Noriker is suitable for working in mountainous areas. It is also used for hauling logs in forests and draft work on farms.

SIZE	15.3–17 hands
ORIGIN	Central Alps, Austria
COLORS	Black, bay, sorrel, gray, spotted

Forelegs are muscular with large joints

Schleswig

The Schleswig was developed in the 19th century as a medium-sized draft horse and was mainly used to pull buses and trams. With an increased use of machines, its demand decreased over time. It is still used on farms and to haul logs and recreational vehicles such as tourist carriages.

SIZE	15.2–16 hands
ORIGIN	Germany
COLORS	Mostly sorrel; also bay, gray

Brabant

Also known as the Belgian Heavy Draft, the Brabant is one of the most influential heavy horse breeds. It was used to develop several European draft breeds. Its calm nature makes it a popular horse.

SIZE	15.2–17 hands
ORIGIN	Belgium
COLORS	Mostly bay, roan; also sorrel, gray

Ardennais

Bred in the 19th century for draft work on farms, the Ardennais was also used in World War I to carry guns and ammunition. Today, it is used in agriculture and is bred for its meat.

Thick legs covered with heavy, coarse feathering _____

Boulonnais

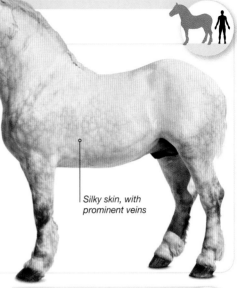

Known for its stamina, the Boulonnais can maintain a steady speed over a long distance. It was originally used in the military, on farms, and for pulling carts, but increased mechanization reduced the demand for horses in these fields of work. Today, it is bred mainly for its meat.

SIZE	14.3–16.3 hands
ORIGIN	Boulogne, France
COLORS	Mostly gray; also black, bay, sorrel

Silky skin, with prominent veins

SIZE	15.1–16.1 hands
ORIGIN	Ardennes, France, and southeast Belgium
COLORS	Mostly bay, roan; also sorrel, gray

Breton

A native horse of northwest France, the Breton is used for draft work in French vineyards. Its strength and stamina make it ideal for agricultural work. It is also crossbred to improve the quality of less developed horses.

SIZE	15.1–16.1 hands
ORIGIN	Black Mountains, France
COLORS	Mostly sorrel; also bay, roan

Percheron

The calm-natured Percheron is one of the breeds used to pull streetcars in Disneyland in the US.

Tough and good-natured, the Percheron is mainly used in transportation and agriculture, and is in demand for its meat. In France, a lighter type of this breed (the Postier) was developed to pull streetcars in Paris.

SIZE   16–17.2 hands

ORIGIN   Normandy, France

COLORS   Gray, black

Norman Cob

For centuries, the Norman Cob has been bred at stud farms in Normandy. Due to crossbreeding, today it is a heavier breed than it originally was. However, it retains its energetic trot, which makes it useful for light draft work on farms.

SIZE 15.3–16.3 hands

ORIGIN La Manche, Normandy, France

COLORS Mostly bay, sorrel; also gray

Limbs are short and muscular

Auxois

Originally, the Auxois was used for transportation and draft work. As demand for this horse decreased due to mechanization, its numbers reduced. Today, it is primarily used to pull wagons and carriages for tourists and is bred for its meat and milk.

SIZE 15.3–16.3 hands

ORIGIN France

COLORS Mostly bay, roan; also sorrel

Muscular thigh with slender legs

Poitevin

For centuries, Poitevin mares have been crossed with donkeys to produce work mules. Their large, wide feet are suited to the marshland they inhabit.

SIZE 16–17 hands

ORIGIN Poitou, France

COLORS Bay, black, dun, gray, sorrel, roan

Italian Heavy Draft

Also known as the Italian Agricultural Horse, this breed was once used extensively for heavy draft work. However, mechanization reduced the need for draft horses, and today it is primarily bred for its meat.

SIZE 15–16 hands

ORIGIN Northern and central Italy

COLORS Mostly sorrel; also bay, roan

Suffolk Punch

This short-legged, broad-chested horse was once used to pull heavy guns during battles. It is immensely powerful, but economical to keep, since it requires less food than other horses of its type and size. It is used in areas with heavy clay soil, and its lack of feathering makes it easy to keep clean. Therefore, it is suitable for heavy farmwork.

SIZE	About 16.1 hands
ORIGIN	Suffolk, England
COLOR	Sorrel

Shire

Known for its strength, the Shire is one of the heaviest draft breeds. This gentle horse is easy to handle, despite its size. It has traditionally been used by brewers to pull wagons loaded with heavy barrels of beer. It is now most often seen in shows and plowing competitions.

SIZE	About 17.2 hands
ORIGIN	Midlands, England
COLORS	Black, brown, bay, gray

Deep girth

Clydesdale

Used mainly for heavy draft work in urban areas, Clydesdales have large, flat feet and a lively, high-stepping knee movement. Most have a white blaze and white markings on the legs, which may sometimes extend to the belly. They are mainly used for shows, farmwork, and riding.

SIZE 16.2 hands

ORIGIN Lanarkshire, Scotland

COLORS Mostly bay, brown; also black, sorrel, gray, roan

American Cream Draft Horse

Developed in the US, this rare breed is known for its distinct color—a cream coat, pink skin, and amber eyes. It was mainly used as a draft breed, but the mechanization of farmwork in the mid-20th century greatly reduced its numbers. However, efforts are being made to increase its population.

SIZE 15–16 hands

ORIGIN US

COLOR Cream

The first engines were compared to the number of horses it would take to pull the same load. Even today, a car engine's performance is measured in

"horsepower"

WORKING HORSE

Before the invention of modern machinery, horses did most of the heavy work on farms—it could take 30 horses to pull one combine harvester. Today, most heavy horses are used in shows, but some people, such as the Amish community in the US, still use horses for farmwork.

Types

Horses can be classified by type as well as breed. Classification as a type is based on the functions that a horse performs, while a horse is classified as a breed based on its conformation. Often, a breed or type is developed in different countries to do a particular job. This means the horses performing this job have similar traits.

RIDING PONY
Because of its calm nature and comfortable riding paces, the riding pony is suitable for child riders.

Types

This category includes horses that are not purebred and do not conform to any breed standard set by breed societies. They have a set of characteristics that help them perform specific functions, such as hunting. They may naturally be of a certain type, or bred for a specific function by crossing suitable individual horses.

Cob

With short, powerful limbs, the Cob has a structure that makes it suitable for carrying weight. Cobs are also often used as show horses in the UK, where they are always hogged (their mane is shaved), as shown here.

SIZE 14.2–15.1 hands

ORIGIN Ireland and England

COLORS All colors

Hunter

The physical features of a Hunter can vary according to the region where it is ridden. For example, in an area with many natural obstacles, such as hedges and streams, a horse with the courage and athletic ability of the Thoroughbred is most suitable. However, all Hunters have great stamina, since they were developed to carry riders across the countryside all day long, following hounds. A typical hunter is bold enough to jump over obstacles in its path.

SIZE More than 14.2 hands

ORIGIN Ireland and UK

COLORS All colors

Well-sloped shoulders are ideal for jumping

Riding Pony

Developed by crossing ponies with small Thoroughbreds, this riding and show horse has the appearance of a pony but the proportions and action of a Thoroughbred.

SIZE	Up to 14.2 hands
ORIGIN	England
COLORS	All colors

Hack

The typical Hack is well-mannered with balanced paces, which makes this type suitable for riding. Hacks used in shows are often crossed with Thoroughbreds, which are known for their elegance.

SIZE	Variable
ORIGIN	England
COLORS	All solid colors

Polo Pony

The most notable feature of a Polo Pony is its compact frame. It has to be fast, agile, and easy to manuever. Thoroughbreds played an important role in the development of this type but the best Polo Ponies come from Argentina, where they are crossed with Criollos.

SIZE	About 15.1 hands
ORIGIN	Argentina
COLORS	Black, brown, bay, sorrel, gray, roan

Strong limbs enable quick turns and sudden stops

Polo was first played by the Persian cavalry, with as many as 100 players on each team

PLAYING POLO

The game of polo originated 2,500 years ago in Persia (modern-day Iran), from where it spread to the rest of Asia. The British established the first official polo club in 1862 in Kolkata, India, and set the rules for the modern game, which is now played by teams of four players. Today, polo is played in around 80 countries.

Famous horses

MYTHICAL HORSES

★ According to Norse mythology, **Sleipnir** is the eight-legged horse of the god Odin. He carries his rider to *Hel*, land of the dead.

★ **Uchchaihshravas** is a seven-headed flying horse in Indian mythology. He is ridden by Indra, the king of heaven.

★ In Greek mythology, **Chiron**, a centaur (half-horse, half-man), is revered for his knowledge of medicine and astrology and considered to be the teacher of Asclepius, the god of medicine.

★ **Pegasus** is a winged horse ridden by the Greek warrior Bellerophon, who defeated the Chimera—a creature with a lion's head, a goat's body, and a serpent's tail—in battle.

★ According to Greek mythology, **Arion** is a divine horse whose father is Poseidon, the god of sea, storms, and horses, and whose mother is Demeter, the goddess of harvest. Arion can speak like a human and is extremely swift.

★ **Kelpie**, a water horse in Celtic mythology, is said to haunt the lakes of Ireland and Scotland. According to legend, it drags its victims under water and drowns them.

HORSES IN LITERATURE

• **Black Beauty**
Anna Sewell's novel *Black Beauty* is about Black Beauty, a horse who narrates his own story. He describes how he was happy and free when young, but how it all changes when he is taken to London to pull cabs.

• **Piebald**
The hero of *National Velvet*, a novel by Enid Bagnold, is 14-year-old Velvet Brown, who rides her horse, Piebald, to victory in the Grand National steeplechase race.

• **Joey**
War Horse, a novel by Michael Morpurgo, tells the story of Joey, a horse taken by the British Army to France to fight in World War I, and his previous owner Albert, who joins the army to try find him.

• **Black Stallion**
Black Stallion is the main character of *The Black Stallion*, a children's book series written by Walter Farley between 1941 and 1989. This 10-book series tells of the many adventures of Black Stallion and his owner, Alec Ramsay.

RECORD BREAKERS

◆ Fastest horse
In 1945, Big Racket completed a quarter-mile (0.4 km) race in 20.8 seconds at a speed of 43.2 mph (69.5 kph).

◆ Tallest and heaviest horse
At a height of 21.2 hands, Mammoth—a Shire born in 1848 in the UK—holds the record for being both the tallest horse and, at 3,360 lb (1,524 kg), the heaviest horse.

◆ Smallest horse
Thumbelina, a dwarf miniature horse born in 2001 in Missouri, stands just 4 hands high.

◆ Oldest horse
A Shire named Old Billy, born in 1760, lived to be 62 years old, the oldest recorded age for a horse. The average lifespan of a horse is about 26 years.

◆ Longest mane
A California mare named Maude had a mane 18 ft (5.5 m) long.

◆ Longest tail
This record is held by an American Palomino named Chinook, whose tail was 22 ft (6.7 m) long.

◆ Most wins
American Thoroughbred Kingston (1884–1912) has won the greatest number of races, with 89 victories between 1884 and 1894. In 1955, he was honored by the United States Racing Hall of Fame.

◆ Most consecutive wins
Camarero (1951–1956), a Thoroughbred racehorse from Puerto Rico, had the highest number of consecutive wins—56 races between 1953 and 1955.

◆ Highest jumper
On February 5, 1949, Huaso (1933–1961), a Chilean Thoroughbred, jumped an 8-ft- (2.47-m-) high obstacle at Vina del Mar in Santiago, Chile. This is the highest jump that has ever been made by a horse.

◆ Longest jumper
Something—who jumped 27½ ft (8.4 m) over water, in Johannesburg, South Africa, on April 25, 1975—holds the record for the longest jump.

◆ Oldest winners
The oldest horses to win a race were three Thoroughbreds: Revenge at Shrewsbury, England, in 1790; Marksman at Ashford, England, in 1826; and Jorrocks at Bathurst, Australia, in 1851.

The Green Monkey, an American Thoroughbred born in 2004, was sold for $16 million—the highest price ever paid for a horse.

All about horses

AMAZING FACTS

♦ As of 2012, there are about **75 million horses** in the world.

♦ Horses **cannot breathe through their mouths** because a flap of tissue blocks the pharynx—the cavity behind the nose that connects the nose and mouth.

♦ The average horse's heart weighs around **8½ lb (3.9 kg)**—that is 12 times the weight of an adult human's heart.

♦ An average 1,000 lb (450 kg) horse drinks around **12 gallons (45 liters)** of water every day—that is 24 times as much as the average human.

♦ The Bashkir is claimed to be the **only hypoallergenic breed**, which means that even people allergic to other horses can ride it. Studies suggest that this is because the Bashkir's hair does not contain the protein that causes allergic reactions.

♦ **Hair from horses' tails** is used for stringing the bows of musical instruments, such as cellos.

♦ A **horse's hoof** grows about ½ in (1 cm) per month.

♦ In official records, **the birthday of all Thoroughbreds** in the northern hemisphere is registered as January 1, and that of all horses in the southern hemisphere as August 1. This makes it easier to keep breeding, racing, and showing records.

♦ The term **"horsepower"** (hp) was coined by the Scottish engineer James Watt to compare the pulling power of a steam engine with that of draft horses. One hp is the power required to carry a weight of 165 lb (75 kg) over a distance of 3¼ ft (1 m) in 1 second.

Equinophobia is the fear of horses. The name comes from the Greek word *phobos*, meaning fear, and the Latin word *equus*, which means horse.

♦ The **age of a horse** can be estimated by looking at its teeth, since its three pairs of incisors appear at different times. Also, over time, the shape of the incisor teeth changes from oval to round, then triangular, and finally square.

♦ There are around **400 different breeds** of the domestic horse.

♦ Horses use their tail to swat flies as well as **to communicate** with each other.

FAMOUS STUD FARMS

The first stud farms were set up in Europe in the 12th century to breed horses for the royal stables and the military. Today, some stud farms are owned by governments, while others are privately owned.

• The National Stud, UK
This is one of the main Thoroughbred stud farms in England. It was established in 1916.

• Le Pin, France
Set up in 1715 as a royal stud farm, it is the oldest of the 20 national breeding farms in France. Its main breeds are Thoroughbred, Percheron, Selle Francais, and French Trotter.

• Piber Federal Stud, Austria
Founded in 1798, this famous farm produces Lipizzaners, some of which are trained at the Spanish Riding School in Vienna, Austria.

• State Stud Celle, Germany
Founded in 1735 by King George II of Britain, this is the main breeding farm of the Hanoverian.

• Kladruby Stud, Czech Republic
One of the oldest breeding farms in the world, this stud farm has been producing the Kladruber since it was founded in 1597 by Emperor Rudolph II (1576–1612).

• Royal Jordanian Stud, Jordan
Founded by King Abdullah I (1921–1946), this is one of the main stud farms in the Middle East for breeding Arabs.

• Calumet Farm, Kentucky
This Thoroughbred stud farm was set up in 1928. It is one of the most famous farms in the Bluegrass Country horse-breeding region of the state of Kentucky.

HORSE FOOD

The natural diet of horses is grass, and they spend much of their time feeding. Working horses are given additional food to provide them with energy, as are growing horses. Some of the most common feeds given to horses have been mentioned below.

★ Grains
Oats are the grain most commonly fed to horses, since they have a high fiber content and are easily digestible.

★ Hay
Fed in bulk as a substitute for grass, hay, unlike most foodstuffs, is usually available to horses at all times, whether in a stable or living out in winter.

★ Complete feeds
These are formulated to provide a balanced diet to horses. There are several types of complete feed. For example, racehorse feeds are made from a very different recipe than pony feeds.

Glossary

Action The way a horse moves.

Ambling A specialized gait in which the horse performs a smooth four-beat leg movement.

Bareback Riding an unsaddled horse.

Brand mark A mark made on the coat of an animal by humans to identify it.

Breed A consistent variety of horse produced by breeding similar types of horse with one another.

Breed society An organization dedicated to a particular breed. It defines the breed standard— the specifications that allow an animal to be classified as that breed. It also records all important dates, news, and activities involving that breed.

Breeding The mating of a male and female animal to produce offspring.

Bridle A type of headgear, usually made of leather, with a metal bit to which the reins are attached.

Cannon The bone between the knee and the fetlock of a hoofed animal.

Carriage horse A horse used to pull wheeled vehicles, such as carriages.

Classical riding A style of riding in which the rider is in complete harmony with the horse, controlling it with minimal movement.

Coldblood A horse from the cold, northern regions of the world.

Conformation The proportions and shape of the skeletal structure and the muscle development of a horse.

Cowboy A person, usually on horseback, who herds and looks after cattle.

Crossbreeding The mating of two different breeds.

Domestication The taming of animals by humans who control their breeding to produce horses with particular characteristics.

Draft Work that involves pulling something heavy, especially vehicles, plows, or other farm machines.

Dressage A kind of competition in which a horse's training and obedience are tested. The horse and its rider are judged on the basis of certain movements that they perform.

Driving An activity in which a horse is attached to a vehicle— such as a wagon, cart, or carriage— in order to pull it.

Endangered At the risk of extinction.

Equestrian Related to horse riding.

Equidae The horse family, which includes horses, zebras, and donkeys.

Eventing A riding competition involving dressage, show jumping, and cross-country.

Evolution The process by which a species may change partially or completely over many generations.

Extinct When a species has no living members, so it has died out.

Feathering Abundant long hair that grows on the fetlocks and covers the hooves.

Feral horses Domesticated horses that have returned to living in the wild.

Fetlock The joint between the cannon and the foot of a horse.

Flehmen The curling of the upper lips by certain animals to examine a smell picked up by the nose.

Foal A horse, or member of the horse family, that is less than one year old.

Fullering A groove on the underside of a horse's shoe.

Gait The pace of a horse—walk, trot, canter, and gallop are the natural gaits of most horses.

Girth The circumference of a horse, measured behind the withers and around the deepest part of the body.

Grooming Cleaning a horse's body and feet.

Hand A unit used to measure the height of a horse. A horse's is measured from the ground to the highest point of the withers. One hand is equal to 4 in (10.16 cm).

Harness A set of straps with which an animal is attached to a vehicle, such as a cart or carriage.

Haulage An activity involving pulling logs or other heavy objects.

Hock A joint on the hind leg of a horse. It is the equivalent of the human ankle.

Horseshoe A shaped shoe attached to the outer edge of a horse's hoof to protect it. Most horseshoes are made of metal.

Hotblood A horse that originated in the desert areas.

In-breeding The mating of closely related animals. It can result in genetic deformities.

Mare A female member of the horse family that is four years old or more.

Markings Natural or human-made marks on an animal's coat.

Marshland A low-lying area that remains flooded or muddy throughout the year.

Moorland An uncultivated hilly area.

Muzzle The part of the horse's head made up of the jaws and nose.

Pack animal An animal used to carry loads rather than a rider.

Play-fighting An activity where animals fight with each other as a game, without the intention of hurting one another.

Primitive Something preserved from an earlier time.

Purebred A horse descended from a line of horses of the same breed.

Quarters The area above the hind legs of an animal that forms the hips.

Ranch A large farm where cattle, horses, and other animals are bred.

Rein A long strap attached to a horse's bridle, used to guide it while riding or driving.

Saddle A seat, usually made of leather, put on the back of an animal for the rider to sit on.

Selective breeding The process by which domesticated animals with desirable traits are bred with each other by humans so that those traits are passed on to their offspring. This may be done to develop a new breed or to improve certain features in existing breeds.

Show horse A type of horse shown in riding classes, such as cobs, hacks, and hunters.

Show jumping A competition sport in which a horse jumps a set course of fences in an arena and collects faults if it refuses or knocks down a jump.

Stallion A male horse that is four years old or more.

Steppe A large area of grassland or semidesert without any trees.

Stirrups Each pair of rings on either side of a saddle, attached to it by a strap. They have flat bases to support the rider's feet.

Stud A stallion used for breeding.

Stud farm A place where horses are bred.

Type A classification of horses according to the activity they are suitable for, rather than their physical features.

Veterinarian A doctor who treats animals.

Warmblood A horse produced by crossbreeding a hotblood and a coldblood.

Western riding A style of horseback riding used by cowboys in the US in which the rider controls the horse with one hand, leaving the other free to hold equipment, such as a lasso.

Withers The top of a horse's shoulders.

Index

Acknowledgments

Dorling Kindersley would like to thank: Monica Byles for proofreading; Helen Peters for indexing; Saloni Talwar and Neha Chaudhary for editorial assistance; and Isha Nagar for design assistance.

The publisher would like to thank the following for their kind permission to reproduce their photographs:

(Key: a-above; b-below/bottom; c-center; f-far; l-left; r-right; t-top)

1 **Dreamstime.com:** Isselee. **2–3 Alamy Images:** Juniors Bildarchiv GmbH. **5 Bob Langrish:** (cl, cr, bc, br). **8 Dreamstime. com:** Terry Alexander (bl). **9 Bob Langrish:** (tr). **13 Dreamstime.com:** Eltoro69 (br). **14 Alamy Images:** Juniors Bildarchiv GmbH (cl, br). **15 Alamy Images:** Juniors Bildarchiv GmbH (tc). **Corbis:** Kit Houghton (tr). **Dreamstime. com:** Carolyne Pehora (b). **16–17 Corbis:** Mike Kemp / In Pictures. **17 Alamy Images:** Kevin Britland (tr). **Getty Images:** Indigo (br). **18 Alamy Images:** Mattphoto (cl). **18–19 Corbis:** Ahmad Sidique / Xinhua Press (c). **19 Dreamstime.com:** Tomas Hajek (br). **Getty Images:** Alan Crowhurst (tr). **20 Alamy Images:** Juniors Bildarchiv GmbH. **22 Alamy Images:** Juniors Bildarchiv GmbH. **23 Alamy Images:** Juniors Bildarchiv GmbH (tr). **Dreamstime.com:** Herman Nel (br); Pavlos Rekas (cl). **24–25 Corbis:** Petr Josek / Reuters. **26 Getty Images:** Dominique Walterson / Flickr. **27 Corbis:** Destinations (bc). **28–29 Alamy Images:** Juniors Bildarchiv GmbH. **29 Corbis:** Kit Houghton (tr). **36–37 Corbis:** (b). **40–41 Bob Langrish:** (t). **42 Fotolia:** CallalooAlexis (tl). **42–43 Dreamstime. com:** Roberto Cerruti (t). **44–45 Corbis:** Bettmann. **46 Dreamstime.com:** Olga Itina (tl). **47 Corbis:** Kit Houghton (tr). **49 Alamy Images:** Tom Salyer. **51 Bob Langrish. 52 Bob Langrish. 53 Bob Langrish:** (br). **55 Corbis:** Kit Houghton. **57 Alamy Images:** John Sylvester (bl). **58–59 Bob Langrish. 60 Alamy Images:** Blickwinkel. **61 Getty Images:** Darrell Gulin / The Image Bank (bc). **62 Alamy Images:** Ilene MacDonald (bl). **62–63 Alamy Images:** Juniors Bildarchiv GmbH. **64 Getty Images:** De Agostini (b). **66–67 Alamy Images:** Blickwinkel (tc). **68 Alamy Images:** Juniors Bildarchiv GmbH. **71 Corbis:** Kit Houghton. **72 Dreamstime.com:** Anduin230. **73 Getty Images:** Claver Carroll / Photolibrary. **76 Dreamstime.com:** Isselee (tl). **76–77 Alamy Images:** Juniors Bildarchiv GmbH (t). **78–79 Alamy Images:** Skyscan Photolibrary. **80–81 Alamy Images:** Juniors Bildarchiv GmbH (t). **82–83 Alamy Images:** Juniors Bildarchiv GmbH (bc). **85 Alamy Images:** Juniors Bildarchiv GmbH (tr). **86 Alamy Images:** Juniors Bildarchiv GmbH. **89 Corbis:** Kit Houghton (tl). **90 Dreamstime.com:** Dinozzo. **91 Corbis:** Kit Houghton. **92–93 Getty Images:** Chris Jackson. **94 Dreamstime.com:** Viktoria Makarova. **95 Bob Langrish:** (br). **96–97 Dreamstime. com:** Alexia Khruscheva. **98 Dreamstime.com:** Viktoria Makarova (tl). **99 Dreamstime.com:** Viktoria Makarova. **100 Dreamstime.com:** Yulia Chupina. **102 Dreamstime.com:** Olga Itina. **103 Alamy Images:** Juniors Bildarchiv GmbH (bl). **104–105 Alamy Images:** Juniors Bildarchiv GmbH (t). **106 Dreamstime. com:** Isselee. **107 Dreamstime.com:** Maria Itina. **109 Alamy Images:** Juniors Bildarchiv GmbH (br). **110–111 Getty Images:** George Rose. **114 Alamy Images:** Juniors Bildarchiv GmbH. **116–117 Alamy Images:** Only Horses Tbk (b). **117 Bob Langrish:** (tr). **118 Corbis:** Kit Houghton. **120–121 Alamy Images:** North Wind Picture Archives. **122 Alamy Images:** Mark J. Barrett. **123 Alamy Images:** Stefan Sollfors (bc). **124–125 Alamy Images:** Juniors Bildarchiv GmbH. **125 Alamy Images:** Mark J. Barrett (tc). **126 Alamy Images:** Ingemar Edfalk (b). **Dreamstime.com:** Jean-louis Bouzou (clb); Verity Johnson (cla). **128 Alamy Images:** Only Horses Tbk (b). **130 Getty Images:** Alain Jocard / AFP. **131 Dreamstime.com:** Martina Berg (bl). **134 Alamy Images:** Mark J. Barrett. **135 Dreamstime.com:** Nancy Kennedy. **136–137 Corbis:** Kevin Fleming. **138 Fotolia:** Samuel René Halifax. **139 fotoLibra :** Jenny Brice (bc). **140 Bob Langrish:** (cb). **144–145 Getty Images:** Andrew Redington.

Jacket images: *Front:* **Dreamstime. com:** Terry Alexander clb/ (White Face), Martina Berg crb/ (Auxois (draft horse)), Jean-louis Bouzou tc/ (Rusty horse shoes); **Getty Images:** Darrell Gulin / The Image Bank tl/ (Cowboys Riding), Indigo cr/ (Wedding of Katie Percy and Patrick Valentine); *Spine:* **Dreamstime.com:** Anastasia Shapochkina t.

All other images © Dorling Kindersley

For further information see: www. dkimages.com